Show Me How to Create
Quilting Designs

70 Ready-To-Use Designs • 6 Projects • Fun, No-Mark Approach

Kathy Sandbach

C&T PUBLISHING

Text and Artwork © 2004 Kathy Sandbach

Publisher: Amy Marson

Editorial Director: Gailen Runge

Editor: Cyndy Lyle Rymer

Technical Editors: Carolyn Aune, Elin Thomas

Copyeditor/Proofreader: Karen Brunson

Cover Designer: Christina Jarumay

Production Artist: Kirstie L. McCormick

Illustrator: Jeff Carrillo, Shawn Garcia, Jay Richards

Production Assistant: Luke Mulks

Photography: Mark Frey unless otherwise noted

Published by C&T Publishing, Inc., P.O. Box 1456, Lafayette,
  California, 94549

Front cover: *Summerhaven* (page 13), designed and made by Maura
Grogan and Judy Gans, quilted by Kathy Sandbach

Back cover: *Nature's Gift* and *View From the Windmill*

Library of Congress Cataloging-in-Publication Data

Sandbach, Kathy.
  Show me how to create quilting designs : 70 ready-to-use designs, 6
projects, fun, no-mark approach / Kathy Sandbach.
    p. cm.
  Includes index.
  ISBN 1-57120-273-0 (paper trade) -- ISBN 1-57120-273-0
  1. Quilting--Design. 2. Quilting--Patterns. 3. Machine quilting. I. Title.

  TT835.S262 2004
  746.46'041--dc22

                              2004001398

Printed in China
10 9 8 7 6 5 4 3 2 1

DEDICATION

This book is dedicated to Diana McClun, Laura
Nownes, Susie Robbins, and Freddy Moran. I
might be lost without their continued friendship,
encouraging words, and gentle pushes to just get
better. Thank you all!

ACKNOWLEDGMENTS

A special thanks to all of my customers: Your
patience, encouragement, lovely pieces, and continued support made this book possible.

Thanks also to my editor, Cyndy Rymer, and all of
the people at C&T for their dedication to publishing books that encourage quilters to reach beyond
their comfort level.

A special thank you to all fabric designers and
artists; Your work is the basis for my inspiration.
Special thanks to Debbie, Carrie, Rick, and Truman
at Golden Valley Nursery in Tracy, California, for
letting me pluck leaves, twigs, and stems for
designs, and to 101 Nursery in Bandon, Oregon,
for letting me do the same.

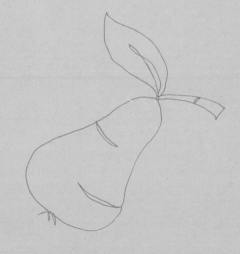

TABLE OF
Contents

Flower Baskets, 45" x 59", designed, pieced, appliquéd, and quilted by the author.

I created this piece using the basket pattern from *Q is for Quilt* and a large floral fabric. I deliberately left lots of empty space for quilting designs, which were all based on the machine appliquéd roses, tulips, lilies, and leaves. My goal was to add more of what was already created with the appliquéd pieces.

Introduction

Most students I meet along the teaching circuit have trouble deciding how to quilt their quilts, and "drawing" designs that please them. As a professional quilter, I discovered easy ways to develop simple designs for machine quilting, which can also be used for hand quilting.

You Don't Need to Draw as Well as Da Vinci

A very basic level of drawing, or what I refer to as a kindergarten level of skill, is all that is needed to translate or create good quilting designs. Most of us have at least that ability. The natural environment, pictures, catalogs, coloring books, and other sources provide many ideas for inspiration. You can easily transform these ideas into wonderful, whimsical, fun, and simple quilting designs. Fabrics are a terrific resource for us all. My first choice is to base quilting designs on the motifs found in the fabrics that were used to compose the quilt. These designs enhance the piecing or appliqué, and create another important level of interest in a quilt. Isn't that what quilting is all about?

Flowers can easily be made into simple quilting designs.

My advice is to think basic. You want the simplest of shapes for quilting. Leave intricate details to the fabric designers, painters, and embroiderers. If you are able to recognize a basic shape, you can create a perfect quilting design.

The Second Stitching Line

I often include a second line of stitching when I quilt. This secondary line of quilting makes it easier to capture the basic nuance or design, is a camouflage for imperfect quilting lines, and provides a second chance to enhance your design or fill the space. Best of all, you can use the second line of stitching to travel gracefully to the next design area.

Note how the second line of quilting helps make the jump to the next design area.

Become a Collector

Start a file of inspiration pieces. Trace around a lovely leaf, or keep a small swatch of fabric that may inspire a quilting design. Children's coloring books are a wonderful source for quilting designs. If you trace or draw a design three or four times with a pencil, you will find it easier to quilt it. Begin to look at shapes with the idea of "drawing with your needle." I do a lot of doodling to find new designs; keep that pad and pencil handy! Most of all, have fun!

CHAPTER 1

Approaching the Design Process

Congratulations, your quilt top is finished! Picking the fabrics was great fun, piecing the wonderful colors together brought the piece alive. Now, for most people, comes the hard part: quilting! For many quiltmakers, this is usually the most difficult part: deciding what to quilt and where to quilt it. For me, this is where the fun begins.

Like many quilters, you probably have several tops that need quilting but have no idea how to quilt them. I firmly believe that the quilting should enhance the pieced or appliquéd design. Don't think of it solely as the glue that holds the layers together. I seldom use all-over designs; instead I prefer to make the designs fit the space, the quilt, and the fabrics.

The most amazing thing happened along my journey of quilting for other people: I found that I did not have to be an artist to "draw" quilting designs! You don't need to be an artist either. All you need is some inspiration and the most basic drawing skills. As with anything else, after a bit of practice, you'll be able to approach the quilting process with eagerness, not a sense of dread.

I encourage students to think about quilting design possibilities while picking not only the fabrics, but also the quilt design itself. Before you begin a quilt, ask yourself these questions:

■ Is the quilt quiltable? Are there 40 points that all converge to one spot? That pile of fabric in one spot is almost impossible to quilt nicely.

■ Are there open spaces for showcasing your quilting? Maybe you can substitute a whole square of fabric for a Nine-Patch block to allow areas where the quilting will be more visible.

■ Is there a sense of motion or a direction to the quilt that you can enhance with quilting? If you have gone to the effort to create a diagonal direction with your piecing, you'll probably want to use quilting to enhance that motion.

■ Think about how you are pressing in relation to the quilting. Are there places where you can stitch in-the-ditch—or what I refer to more simply as ditching—using a beige or other neutral-colored thread instead of invisible nylon thread (nylon is always my last choice of thread) if you press in a different direction? Pressing should be neatly done. I recommend not opening your seams if you plan to do ditch quilting. With open seams there is no "ditch," which makes quilting the seamline almost impossible.

■ Pick fabrics that you can use for inspiration, such as a fun frog fabric or a wonderful floral design that can be quilted. Choosing fabrics for the quilting enhances the entire piece.

We Are All Artists

So you think you aren't an artist just because you can't draw a rose, a horse, a cow, or a maple leaf without help. Don't give up! Here are some ideas that I use every day for inspiration. I do not copy someone else's drawing, picture, or artwork, but I do use their expertise and artistic designs to create basic shapes for quilting.

Don't Recycle Those Catalogs Just Yet

I'll wager that you received at least a dozen new catalogs in the mail this week. Pick up one and leaf through it, to look for possible quilting ideas. Don't get distracted by the clothes or lovely garden supplies; stay focused on looking for simple shapes that may translate to quilting designs. Home decor pieces, a lapel pin, or a dramatic design on a rug are just a couple of suggestions. In one of my classes, a student was wearing a dress with wonderful whimsical giraffes all over it; what a great idea for quilting!

Go to Your Stash

You probably have hundreds (if not thousands) of fabric pieces on your shelves, in drawers, baskets, boxes, under the bed, and so on. Your fabric collection will most likely yield many wonderful quilting designs. If you have a piece of fabric that features different types of butterflies, you'll soon realize a butterfly's wings come in many different shapes. It's easy to develop a half dozen different butterfly quilting patterns from that one piece of fabric.

Butterfly fabric

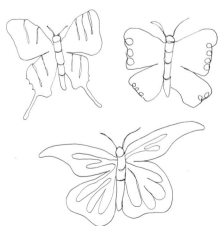

Butterfly quilting designs

Fabric manufacturers tell me that approximately 80 percent of printed fabrics include flowers, leaves, or other shapes inspired by the natural world. I'll bet you have fabric with flowers such as roses, tulips, hibiscus, or poppies; or cyclamen, oak, or maple leaves; or other natural designs. Inspiration! Speaking of inspiration, how about this wonderful collection of teapots that easily translate into quilting designs.

Teapot fabric

Teapot quilting designs

Head Outside

Take a walk through your local park or on a nature path of some sort. There are probably at least a dozen different leaf shapes to use as inspiration for quilting designs. You may even have a half dozen different trees in your own backyard. There are dozens of interesting leaf shapes out there! Visit your local nursery and look at the leaf shapes; there are hundreds waiting to be discovered and quilted!

Just the Basics

Sounds simple, but it is true: In quilting designs, you need just the basic shape. In quilting, you only need to capture what I refer to as the "basic nuance" of a shape for quilting. For example, if I quilt the first design below, can you guess what it is? It could be an apple, a pumpkin, a cherry, or . . . ? If I quilt the second design, you absolutely know it is an apple! You can certainly find perfectly round apples and pictures or fabric with perfectly round apples. However, it is the shading, perspective, color, and drawing that make it an apple. We don't need that kind of detail for quilting; maybe in embroidery work, but definitely not in quilting.

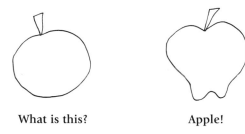

What is this?   Apple!

So think basic. This is what I call the recognizable shape, and it is often the smallest curve or nuance that will make it recognizable.

Double-Line Quilting

The designs I create for quilting have just enough detail to make them identifiable, but are really stripped down to the basic shape. I use lots of double-line quilting to convey the basic shape and to create another point of interest. I try to create a "ribboned" effect, not a double-needle look. The second stitching line adds a sketch-like quality to the drawing. Guess what: A sketch needs to be a lot less perfect than a single-line drawing. This allows more room for expanding the drawings, and for

possibly correcting a poor shape. It also allows you to cross over a jagged line created the first time through, or helps you travel to the next design in a row or border.

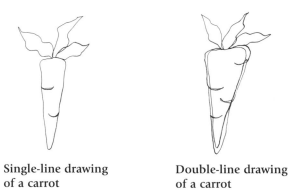

Single-line drawing   Double-line drawing
of a carrot   of a carrot

Thread Color

The color of thread you choose also helps make the design identifiable. The three designs below are almost the same, but the color shows the first is an orange, the second is a lemon, and the third is a lime.

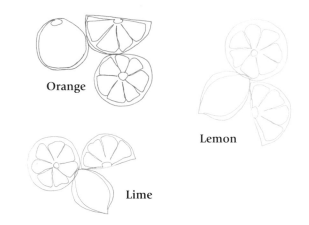

Orange

Lemon

Lime

Location quilting is also a big help in the identifying process. Quilting a very simple daffodil shape right next to the daffodil fabric will help make your design recognizable.

Creating Designs

Here are my three basic goals for quilting designs.

1. Create an identifiable design.

2. Create a continuous-line design so you can eliminate as many starts and stops as possible.

3. Try to fill the space while working in a particular area. By doing so you don't have to return to the same space, and it also helps save starts and stops. For example, if a flower doesn't fill the space, add some leaves, stems, or twigs. Double-line quilting also helps fill up the empty spaces.

Fill the space with quilting.

Before quilting a design, I start with paper and pencil to create a drawing that is quiltable and recognizable. It usually takes four or five attempts before I have a design. Next, I practice quilting until the shape pleases me and suggests the shape I want. If size is a problem, then I draw a square or other shape that corresponds to the size I need on my quilt and practice filling in the space.

Density

Filling a space evenly is very important. You don't want a design with very dense quilting or nine lines that all converge at one spot.

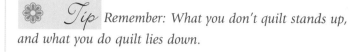 *Tip Remember: What you don't quilt stands up, and what you do quilt lies down.*

The aim in every design you create is an even distribution of quilted space versus unquilted space.

Too much quilting   **A balanced quilting design**

Use just enough lines to make your drawing identifiable. The photo of a bicycle shows lots of detail, but the drawing boils it down to just a couple of wheels, a bit of a frame, a seat, and handlebars. Did you notice that with the double-line quilting, a third line here and there isn't noticeable?

Bicycle   **Drawing of a bicycle**

Like Your Piano Teacher Used to Tell You

Practice is the key to successful quilting. Repeatedly quilting the same design helps you perfect a drawing. Remember, think BASIC!

CHAPTER 2

Supplies & Tips

Your Sewing Machine

Your sewing machine should be kept in excellent working order. Have it serviced at least once a year, and more often if you use it heavily. I do not have a longarm quilting machine, nor do I use any of the setups that I call longarm wanna-bes. I do allover designs very seldom. Longarm machines can limit the flexibility to quilt by block or section or around a border in a continuous line. The machine I use is a Brother 1500S, which has a much bigger space to the right of the needle than many machines do. It is also quite a bit faster than a regular domestic machine and has many advantages for machine quilters. The next time you're in the market for a machine, consider what you'll be using it for and all of the features that are necessary for your use.

Best Foot Forward

I do all quilting, including straight lines and ditching, with a darning foot or free-motion foot. The smaller the darning foot, the better; the smaller foot creates the best compression at the point where you're stitching, which makes a better stitch. With a small darning foot, it is less likely that your thread will break or your machine will skip a stitch. It doesn't seem to make much difference whether the foot is clear plastic or metal, open or closed. Visibility is not a factor, because you should be looking ahead of where the needle is, not at the needle. Most of the machines on the market today have multiple choices in darning feet; pick the smallest!

Thread

I use Aurifil's 50-weight Mako cotton almost exclusively for machine quilting. This is a lovely Egyptian cotton, strong and almost lint-free (which makes your machine much happier). With all the double stitching lines that I do, I think the lighter-weight thread looks better than the heavier threads do. I use many variegated threads, as well as solids. The Aurifil thread also works well in the bobbin when I use metallic or nylon on the top. I no longer use rayon or polyester to machine quilt, because I found that the thread ends (the starts and stops) were "fuzzing out" on the tops of my quilts. Manufacturers tell me that rayon and polyester threads were designed for embroidery work, in which all the starts and stops are on the back side. When I want a heavier thread, I often use YLI 40-weight mercerized cotton quilting thread or Aurifil's 28-weight cotton. My collection of threads is very simple; with a light and dark thread in all of the basic colors, I have almost every thread color that I need for quilting virtually any quilt.

Needle Size

Needle size is an important factor in machine quilting. I use a 90/14 most of the time. This is a bit big for some threads, but I never have to worry about the needle breaking or the thread shredding. Change your needle regularly and, of course, make sure you use a sharp, top-stitch, quilting, or jeans needle. Never use a universal needle for quilting.

Batting

Batting should be cotton or mostly cotton. Thick polyester batting does not machine quilt well. Warm and Natural is my favorite because of its consistent thickness and because it pieces beautifully. It machine quilts extremely well, hangs perfectly, and washes without shrinkage. (Don't put your quilt in the dryer; if you do, use low heat and dry it for only ten minutes or so.) As long as you use first-quality cotton or mostly cotton batting, your machine quilting will look great.

Gloves

You really need to wear gloves while machine quilting. After using rubber fingers for many years, I switched to gloves because the rubber grips on the face of the gloves

greatly increase my control while quilting. The gloves I prefer are Quilt Gripper Gloves, which are knitted from lightweight cotton and are easy to put on and take off. They are lightweight enough that you can change bobbins and thread your needle without removing them. I have found that anything rigid, such as hoops or discs, will impair the movement of the quilt while quilting. Most of us don't have as much space as we would like to the right of the needle, and certainly we don't want to give up any of the space we do have. Using a rigid tool to hold the quilt compromises that space. With gloves, you can maintain a flat, taut, smooth surface while quilting your designs.

Repositioning your hands with the machine stopped will help you create quilting lines without jogs or jagged motion. I tell my students to consider their hands as the hoop that holds the fabric flat and taut and moves it smoothly. I recommend that the hands be positioned in a U-shape.

Basting

Good basting, with a well-pieced back that is freshly pressed and taped down on a hard surface for pin-basting, will help the appearance of your quilting. I prefer size 0 solid brass safety pins for basting because they are much easier to open and close than steel pins. Never use a pin larger than size 2, because larger pins may create holes in your fabric. Pins placed approximately 5" to 6" apart in every direction will secure your quilt nicely, regardless of the size of the pins.

Stitch Length

Stitch length is very important to achieving a really nice look in your quilting. Ten or twelve stitches per inch look great. If you have four stitches or twenty stitches per inch, your tension will be very poor, because our domestic machines are not really designed for these extremes of stitching. Good tension can be achieved only with about eight to fourteen stitches per inch; don't blame your machine for tension problems if you have great large stitches or little bitty ones. Practice is the key to even, small stitches.

CHAPTER 3

Projects

Following are six projects for you to try. Each relies on the flowers, leaves, or food in the fabrics for quilting inspiration. All the fabrics for these projects were chosen with quilting in mind. The visibility factor was, of course, important for the photographs in the book. If you are fairly new to machine quilting, your choice of fabrics will probably not be quite so solid looking as those in the projects. With tone-on-tone fabrics and busier prints, the quilting is less visible and more forgiving and will act as a camouflage. If you want your quilting to truly stand out, your fabric needs to read as a solid or almost solid, and quilting thread should be a high-contrast color.

Finished quilt size: 64" x 72"
Designed and pieced by Maura Grogan, Tucson, AZ, and Judy Gans, Sudbury, MA, 2003.
Quilted by the author.

Fabrics

2 large scale prints: 1½ yards total

2 or 3 greens: 1 yard total

2 or 3 pinks: 1¼ yards total

2 or 3 oranges: ¾ yard total

2 or 3 golds: 1⅜ yards total

2 or 3 reds: 1 yard total

Black: 2¾ yards (includes binding)

Backing: 4 yards

Batting: 69" x 77"

If you want to create your own design, a couple of hints might help you. Start with a line drawing of the quilt and colored pencils. This piece began with a "frame" of sorts using the solid black. Then the large triangles of green were placed. Notice that *Summerhaven* has a green diagonal rectangle that allowed me to vine quilt a large wavy-edged catalpa leaf. Cut and place your other fabrics to fill the space with a balance of color.

There are two basic "pie" shapes or one-eighth-circle shapes: one large and one small. These help soften all the strong angles in this quilt. Cut and place some of your large prints, using the wedges, to get a feel of their weight in the whole project. You will want to fussy cut the large prints so you can center the flowers.

Stand back and view your piece from a distance or, better yet, use a reducing glass. This view gives you a sense of the balance and helps you select colors for each space.

Cutting

🌸 *Note* *This quilt follows a design-as-you-go approach. Start by cutting some of each shape and placing them on your design wall.*

1. Begin by cutting some black squares 8½" x 8½" and some black squares 8⅞" x 8⅞", then cut the 8⅞" squares diagonally into triangles. (Maura and Judy's quilt uses 3 black squares and 24 black triangles.)

2. To make the green diagonal rectangle shape, cut squares 8⅞" x 8⅞", then cut diagonally into triangles. (Maura and Judy's quilt uses 18 green triangles.)

3. Cut additional squares 8⅞" x 8⅞", then cut diagonally into triangles from red and large-print fabrics.

4. Make plastic templates for pieces A–D, located on the pullout. Using the templates, cut large print and solid pie shapes and backgrounds. Remember that you will need to cut half of the backgrounds in reverse. Arrange the pie shapes, backgrounds, and additional triangles to fill in the space of your quilt.

5. Cut 8 black strips 2¼" wide for the binding.

Quilt Assembly

1. Sew the A or C pie-shaped pieces into pairs. Remember that you are working with bias edges. Very gently press the seams to one side.

2. Sew the B and Br, or the D and Dr, background pieces together. Press the seams in the opposite direction of the pie wedges.

3. Carefully pin the pie shapes to the B/Br, or the D/Dr, background pieces. Sew together, placing the pie piece on the bottom when sewing. Press toward the pie.

Pin and sew pie unit to background unit.   **Press toward pie shapes.**

4. Sew the triangles into squares, then sew all the squares into rows. Press alternate rows in opposite directions.

5. Sew the rows together and press.

6. Layer the quilt top, batting, and backing, and baste.

Finishing
Quilting

First I ditched around the circles, then the border and pale green triangles that create the floating rectangle. The flowers and leaves in the large prints inspired the decorative quilting designs. The flowers included a big dahlia-type flower, a rose, and a sort of indistinct poppy. I quilted the flowers with three or four different thread colors. I randomly placed the quilted flowers in the pieced areas and along the border. Then I quilted leaves to fill in the rest. Notice I more or less double-stitched all the flowers and added a third row of quilting around them with the green thread while I was adding the leaves, sticks, and curls. Again, there are no rules here, just quilt as you wish, using the fabrics to inspire quilting designs: big leaves, small leaves, big and small flowers, quarter, half, or three-quarter flowers.

Binding

1. Sew the binding strips together. Press in half lengthwise.

2. Sew the binding to the front of the quilt. Fold the binding to the back and hand stitch in place.

Quilt Layout Diagram

Summerhaven Quilting Designs

Finished quilt size: 35" x 42"
Designed and pieced by Anelie Belden, Volcano, CA. Quilted by the author.

Fabrics

Anelie chose lavenders, purples, and plums, but this would also look great in shades of greens, yellows, or golds.

Lights: 6 or 8 to total 1¼ yards for backgrounds

Darks: 6 or 8 to total 1½ yards for darker focus squares and appliquéd leaves

Border: ⅝ yard

Binding: ½ yard

Backing: 1⅜ yards

Batting: 40" x 47"

Lightweight paper-backed fusible web (18" wide): 1⅜ yards

Cutting

🌸 *Note You may choose to cut squares and triangles a few at a time, and follow a design-as-you-go approach.*

Lights

Cut 31 squares 4" x 4".

Cut 19 squares 4⅜" x 4⅜", then cut diagonally to make 38 triangles.

Cut 6 squares 3⅛" x 3⅛", then cut diagonally to make 12 triangles.

Darks

From each of 2 dark fabrics, cut 4 squares 4" x 4".

From each of the same 2 dark fabrics, cut 4 squares 4⅜" x 4⅜", then cut diagonally to make 8 triangles.

From each of 7 dark fabrics, cut 2 squares 4⅜" x 4⅜", then cut diagonally. You will need 22 triangles total.

From each of 3 dark fabrics, cut a square 2½" x 2½" for the Square-Within-a-Square blocks.

From 1 dark fabric, cut 4 squares 2½" x 2½".

From each of 3 dark fabrics, cut 2 squares 4" x 4" for border triangles (do not cut into triangles yet).

Border

🌸 *Note Before cutting the border, measure your quilt and adjust the border lengths if necessary.*

Left border: Cut 1 strip 4" x 32" and 1 square 4" x 4".

Right and top borders: Cut 2 strips 4" x 28½" and 2 strips 4" x 7½" each.

Bottom border: Cut 1 strip 4" x 35½".

Binding

Cut 5 strips 2¼" wide x the width of the fabric.

Quilt Assembly

1. To make the 3 small Square-Within-a-Square blocks, sew 2 light 3⅛" triangles to opposite sides of a dark 2½" square. Press toward the dark. Add 3⅛" triangles to the remaining sides. Press. Repeat to make 2 more Square-Within-a-Square blocks.

Sew triangles to 2 sides and add remaining triangles.

Square-Within-a-Square block
Make 3.

2. To make the small square in the second and third rows of the quilt, place a 2½" dark square on the corner of a 4" light square. Sew on the diagonal of the small square, as shown. Trim the corner and press toward the dark. Repeat with 2 additional light 4" squares.

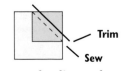

Sew on the diagonal and trim.   Press. Make 3.

3. In the same manner, sew a 2½" dark square on the corner of a 4⅜" light triangle. Trim the corner and press.

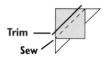

Press. Make 1.

4. Using the quilt photo and the diagram on page 20 arrange the dark and light triangles and squares, the 3 pieced squares with the pieced triangle (placed together), and the Square-Within-a-Square blocks on your design wall.

5. Sew the triangles into squares, then sew into rows. Press alternate rows in opposite directions.

6. Sew rows together and press.

7. To make the left border, place a dark 4" x 4" square on one end of the 4" x 32" strip. Sew along the diagonal of the square, making sure the diagonal goes in the correct direction. Trim the corner and press. Repeat, using a dark 4" x 4" square and a border 4" x 4" square. Sew the border segments together and press. Sew to the left side of the quilt and press toward the border.

Left Border

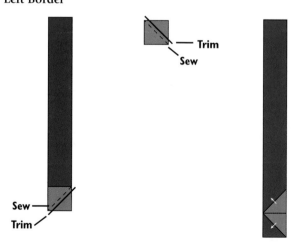

8. To make the right and top borders, place a square on one end of a 4" x 28½" strip and sew along the diagonal of the square as you did for the left border. Repeat for the 4" x 7½" strip. Be sure to check the direction of the diagonal as you piece the strips. Sew the border segments together and press.

Right Border

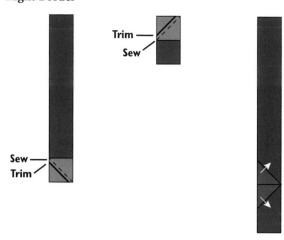

Top Border

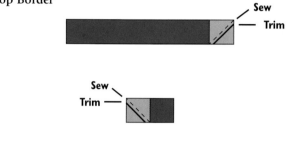

9. Sew the side border to the right of the quilt and press toward the border. Sew the top border to the top of the quilt and press.

10. Sew the 4" x 35½" strip to the bottom of the quilt. Press toward the border.

Quilt Layout Diagram

Appliqué

1. Trace the leaf designs, located on the pullout, onto the paper side of the fusible web and cut out the shapes, leaving ½" or so outside the lines.

2. Following the manufacturer's directions, fuse the web shapes to the wrong side of the fabric. Cut out on the lines.

3. Peel the paper off the leaves, and using the quilt photo as a guide, place the leaves onto the quilt top. Fuse in place.

4. Machine appliqué the shapes to the background. Anelie used a buttonhole stitch.

5. Layer the quilt top, batting, and backing, and baste.

Finishing

Quilting

Begin by ditching around the squares and the border. Outline stitch around the appliquéd leaves, quilting some veins on the leaves as well. Use contrasting threads to add quilted leaves and vines in the background and borders.

Binding

1. Sew the binding strips together. Press in half lengthwise.

2. Sew the binding to the front of the quilt. Fold the binding to the back and hand stitch in place.

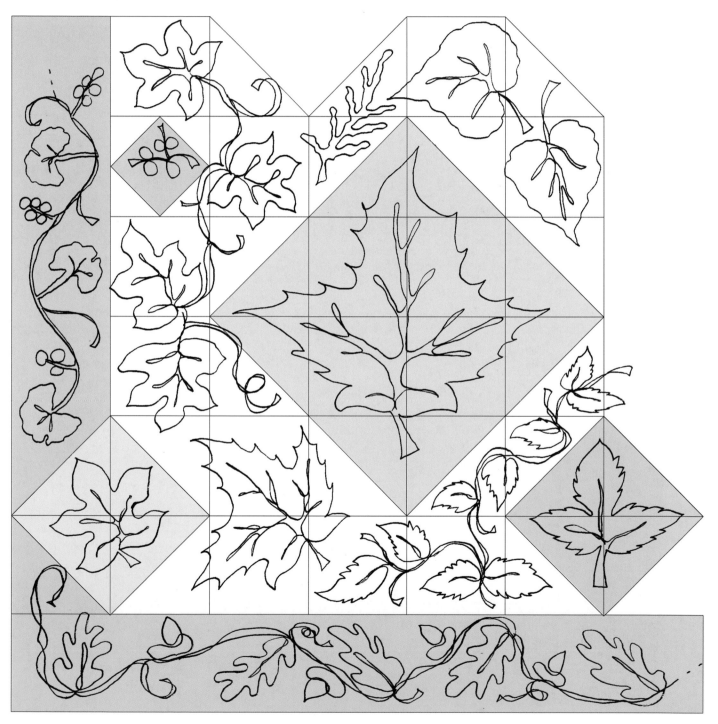

Nature's Gift Quilting Designs

Finished quilt size: 50" x 55"
Designed, pieced, and appliquéd by Susie Robbins, Vallejo, CA. Quilted by the author.

Fabrics

Solid black: 2⅞ yards for background, borders, and binding

Floral prints: ½ yard each of 2 fabrics for appliquéd flowers

Leaf print: 2 yards for bias vines and appliquéd leaves

Light-green solid: ¼ yard for half-square triangles

Purple print: ⅜ yard for inner border

Backing: 3¼ yards

Batting: 55" x 60"

Lightweight paper-backed fusible web (18" wide): 4 yards

Washable fabric marker or chalk

Cutting

🌸 *Note* *Before cutting the borders, measure your quilt and adjust the border lengths if necessary.*

Black

Cut 1 rectangle 34½" x 39½" for center.

Cut 2 strips 1⅞" x the width of the fabric for the half-square triangles.

Cut 6 strips 5" x the width of the fabric for the outer border. Piece as necessary, and cut 2 side borders 5" x 46½" and top and bottom borders 5" x 50½".

Cut 8 strips 1½" x the width of the fabric for the inner and third borders, then cut into strips the following lengths:

- Left inner border: 25½" and 3½"
- Right inner border: 29½" and 4½"
- Top inner border: 28½" and 1½"
- Bottom inner border: 21½", 8½", and 2½"
- Left third border: 21", 10½", and 3"
- Right third border: 13", 7", 5½", 4", and 3"
- Top third border: 19", 6½", 5", and 3½"
- Bottom third border: 12", 11½", 4", and 7"

Cut 6 strips 2¼" wide for the binding.

Leaf Print

Fold fabric in half diagonally to form a bias edge. Cut bias strips 1½" wide x approximately 12 yards (432") total for bias vines.

Light-Green Solid

Cut 2 strips 1⅞" x width of the fabric.

Purple Print

Cut 4 strips 2" x width of the fabric. Cut into 2 strips 2" x 41½", and 2 strips 2" x 39½".

Quilt Assembly

🌸 *Note* *The vines are all different lengths, and the ends will be either knotted or covered by appliqué, so there is no need to piece the vine strips into a long piece that is more difficult to handle.*

1. Fold the bias vine strips in half lengthwise, with right sides together. Sew using a ⅛" seam allowance.

2. Turn strips right side out. Press the seam down the center of the back.

3. Press the fusible web to the wrong side of the floral fabrics and the remainder of the leaf fabric, following the manufacturer's directions.

4. Carefully cut out the designs, following the outline of the printed flowers and leaves. You will need about 25 assorted flowers and 60 assorted leaves.

5. With a marker or chalk, mark a circle 23" in diameter at the center of the black rectangle. Use this circle and the photo as guides to create your central wreath.

6. Knot the exposed ends of your vine strips and appliqué the vine in place, either by hand or machine. Peel the paper off the flowers and leaves and place along the vine. Fuse and machine-buttonhole in place, or use quilting to hold in place.

7. Layer the light-green and black 1⅞" strips with right sides together. Cut 36 squares 1⅞" x 1⅞", then cut them diagonally into 72 triangles. Sew into 71 half-square triangles (you will not use one triangle). Press toward the black.

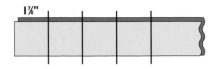

Layer black and green strips.

Cut diagonally.   Sew.   Press toward black.

8. Piece the half-square triangles and the 1½"-wide black inner border strips following the quilt layout diagram on page 25. Press seams toward the black strips. Add to the sides and top and bottom of the quilt center and press toward the center.

9. Add the purple border to the sides and then the top and bottom of the quilt. Press toward the purple border.

10. Piece together more of the half-square triangles and the 1½" wide black third border strips and add to the sides and then the top and bottom of the quilt top. Press toward the purple border.

11. Add the black outer borders to the sides and then the top and bottom of the quilt top. Press toward the outer border.

12. Using the photo as a guide, appliqué more vines, leaves, and flowers around the borders.

13. Layer the quilt top, batting, and backing, and baste.

Finishing

Quilting

Start by quilting colored flowers inspired by the appliquéd pieces. Add these in the center and the four inner corners, using a double line of quilting. Fill the remaining space with a vine of *Susie's split leaf* (see design on page 45), or a leaf of your own choosing, and add sticks and curls, outlining the appliquéd flowers in green. It really is a simple process of following the outline of the flowers, then following the vine and filling the spaces with leaves, sticks, and curls.

Binding

1. Sew the binding strips together. Press in half lengthwise.

2. Sew the binding to the front of the quilt. Fold the binding to the back and hand stitch in place.

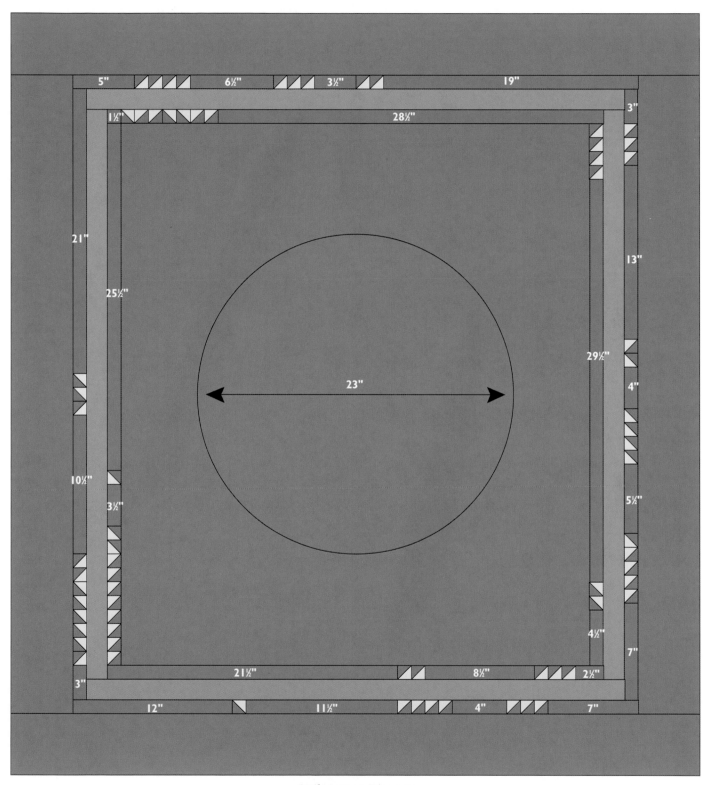

Quilt Layout Diagram

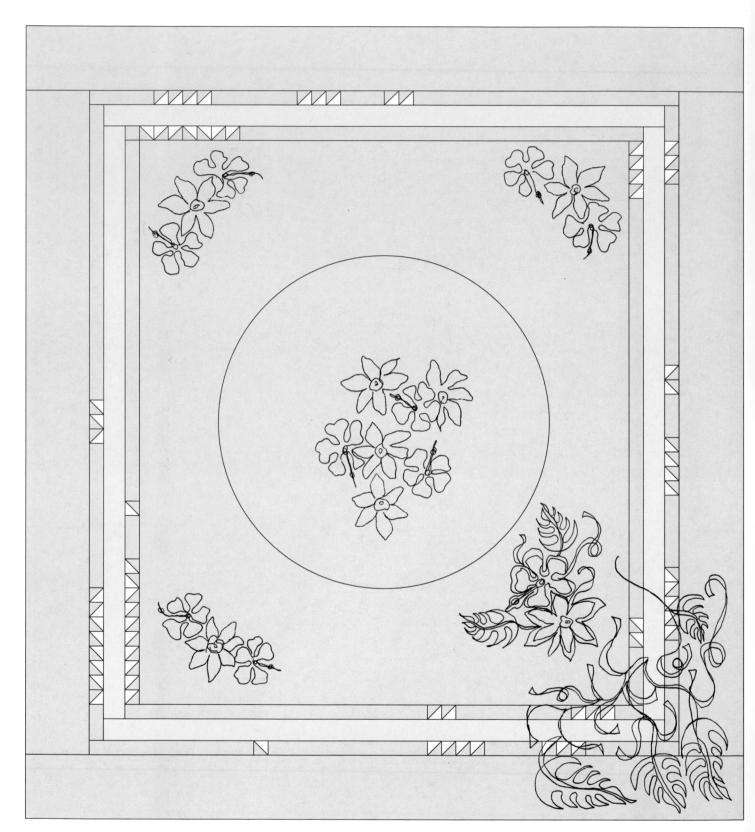

View From the Windmill Quilting Designs

Finished quilt size: 31½" x 36"
Designed, pieced, and quilted by the author.

Finished quilt size: 31½" x 36"

Designed, pieced, and quilted by the author

Fabrics

🌸 *Note* *The amounts listed are enough for one wallhanging.*

Light: ½ yard for background

Fruit or vegetable fabric: ½ yard for border squares

12 to 15 different bright colors and fruit or vegetable fabrics: 2" x 21" strips of each for the Nine-Patch blocks (¾ to 1 yard total)

Black-and-white polka-dot: ⅝ yard for lattice, inner border, and binding

Backing: 1¼ yards

Batting: 36" x 41"

Lightweight paper-backed fusible web (18" wide): 1 yard

Cutting

Light

Cut 3 strips 4½" wide, then cut into 5 strips 20½" long for background.

🌸 *Note* *Before cutting the borders, measure your quilt and adjust the border lengths if necessary.*

Polka-Dot

Cut 2 strips 1⅝" wide, then cut into 4 strips 20½" long for lattice.

Cut 3 strips 1¾" wide, then cut into 2 strips 20½" long and 2 strips 27½" long for inner border.

Cut 4 strips 2¼" wide for the binding.

Fruit or Vegetable Fabric

Cut 2 strips 5" wide, then cut strips into 13 squares 5" x 5" for border squares.

Appliqué

1. Trace the fruit or vegetable designs, located on the pullout, onto the paper side of the fusible web and cut out the shapes, leaving ½" or so outside the lines. Reverse some of the stems and pieces to add variety to your project.

2. Following the manufacturer's directions, fuse the web to the wrong side of the fabric and cut out on the lines.

3. Peel the paper off the designs and fuse them onto the background fabric, using the photo as a guide.

4. Machine appliqué the shapes to the background. I used a machine buttonhole stitch.

🌸 *Note* *It will be much easier to do the machine buttonhole work before piecing the rows together.*

Quilt Assembly

1. Sew a 1⅝"-wide polka-dot lattice strip between the appliqué strips. Press the seams toward the polka-dot strip.

2. Sew the 1¾" x 20½" polka-dot inner border strips to the top and bottom of the quilt top. Press. Add the 1¾" x 27½" inner border strips to the sides. Press.

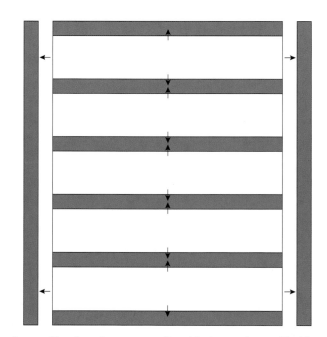

Sew polka-dot pieces to appliquéd pieces, then add sides.

3. Mix the bright-colored and fruit (or vegetable) fabric 2"-wide strips into sets of 3 strips; sew together along the long edge. Press seam allowances to one side; cut strips into 2" segments.

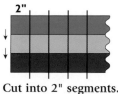

Cut into 2" segments.

4. Sew the segments into Nine-Patch blocks. Press. You need a total of 13 blocks.

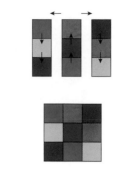

Make 13 Nine-Patch blocks.

5. Alternate three Nine-Patch blocks with three 5" fruit or vegetable fabric squares for the side borders and sew together. Press toward the 5" squares. Add to the sides of the quilt. Press toward inner border.

6. Alternate Nine-Patch blocks with fruit or vegetable fabric squares, press, and sew to the top and bottom of the quilt. Press.

7. Layer the quilt top, batting, and backing, and baste.

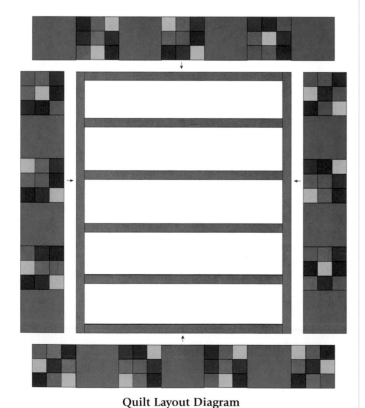

Quilt Layout Diagram

Finishing
Quilting

Begin by ditch quilting; because of the way the seams are pressed, it is easy to ditch all of the appliqué panels and then move on to the decorative pieces. Outline quilt the appliqué shapes with color-coordinated threads. Using the appliquéd fruit or vegetable shapes as inspiration, fill the spaces with more fruits or vegetables, or add to what was already appliquéd. Use a coordinating thread, which helps to make your quilting designs recognizable. Remember to use double-line stitching to enhance your designs and to balance the space. Fruit and Vegetable quilting designs are on pages 57–62.

The border quilting is not really visible because of the busy fabrics. I first ditched between the squares of food fabrics and the Nine-Patch blocks. Add more fruits or vegetables in the Nine-Patches, then add stakes that you might see in a garden with the names of the fruits or vegetables.

Use words such as "Farmers' Market" or "fresh, organically grown fruits and vegetables" or "locally grown" to quilt the inner borders. Add rows of words such as "apples, apples, apples" between the appliqué rows.

Binding

1. Sew the binding strips together. Press in half lengthwise.

2. Sew the binding to the front of the quilt. Fold the binding to the back and hand stitch in place.

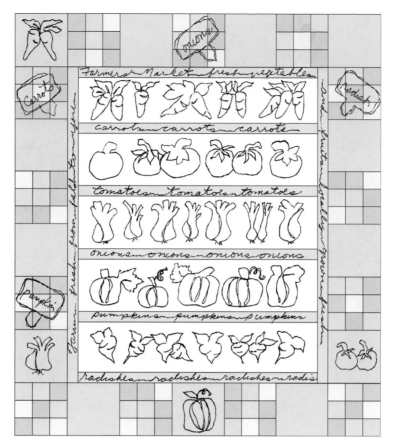

Vegetable quilting designs

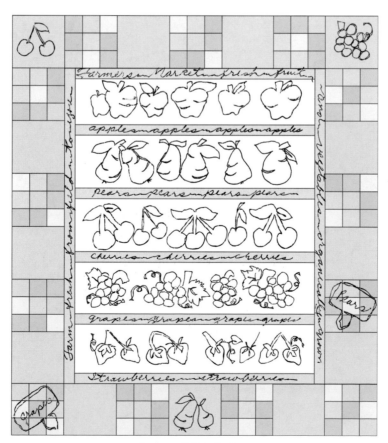

Fruit quilting designs

Finished size: 15" x 22" each
Designed, pieced, and quilted by the author.

Placemats

Fabrics

❀ *Note Even though the food fabric piece is narrow, you will need ½ yard for directional prints so the print will be upright on the placemat. If you use non-directional prints and a different fabric for the backing, ¼ yard is sufficient.*

For each placemat, you will need the following:

Food fabric: ½ yard (I used apples, cherries, citrus, and pears, but there are dozens of food fabrics at your local quilt shop, and quilting designs for many of them at the back of this book. Feel free to create your own quilting designs based on the food you choose.)

Coordinating solid or semi-solid fabric: ½ yard

Backing: ½ yard

Black: ¼ yard for binding

Batting: 17" x 24"

Freezer paper

❀ *Note If you choose to use the leftover coordinating solid or food fabric for the backing, you will not need to purchase additional backing fabric.*

Cutting

Food Fabric

Cut a strip 5½" x 15½".

Solid

Cut a rectangle 15½" x 17½".

Backing

Cut a rectangle 17" x 24".

Black

Cut 2 strips for binding 2¼" wide x the width of the fabric.

Placemat Assembly

1. Sew the food fabric strip to the solid rectangle. Press seam toward the food fabric.

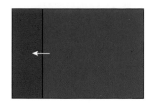

2. Layer placemat top, batting, and backing, and baste.

Finishing

Quilting

1. Trace the quilted word designs, located on the pull-out, onto the dull (not shiny) side of the freezer paper.

2. Cut out the words and iron them onto the layered placemat.

3. Quilt around the freezer paper letters close to the edge, but not on it. Gently peel away the paper and quilt to fill in the overlapping parts of the letters. Add the fruit above and below the words. To make the starts and stops invisible, I left long threads—I pulled them to the back, knotted them, and cut short tails. Food quilting designs are on pages 57–62. Quilt the food fabric following the outlines of the fabric print.

Binding

1. Sew the binding strips together. Press in half lengthwise.

2. Sew the binding to the front of the quilt. Fold the binding to the back and hand stitch in place.

Let's Eat! Placemat Quilting Designs

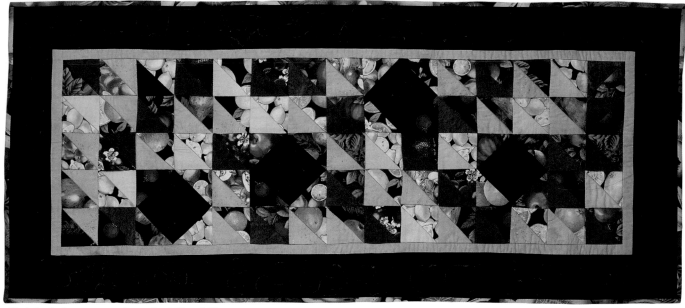

Finished size: approximately 24" x 54"
Designed, pieced, and quilted by the author.

Table Runner

Fabrics

Food fabrics: 4 to 6 assorted to total ⅝ to ¾ yard plus an additional ⅜ yard for binding

Coordinating solids or semisolids: 4 to 6 assorted to total ⅝ to ¾ yard

Solid or semisolid: ¼ yard for the inner border

Black: ¾ yard for outer border and triangles

Backing: 1⅝ yards

Batting: 29" x 59"

Cutting

❀ *Note* *Before cutting the borders, measure your table runner and adjust the border lengths if necessary.*

Food Fabrics

Cut 4 strips 3⅞" wide x width of the fabric, then cut the strips into squares 3⅞" x 3⅞". Cut the squares on the diagonal to make a total of 75 food fabric triangles.

Cut 5 strips 2¼" wide x width of the fabric for the binding.

Solids

Cut 4 strips 3⅞" wide x the width of the fabric, then cut the strips into 3⅞" x 3⅞" squares. Cut the squares on the diagonal to make a total of 59 solid triangles.

Cut 4 strips 1½" wide for the inner border. Piece if necessary, then cut into 2 strips 1½" x 15½" and 2 strips 1½" x 45½".

Black

Cut 1 strip 3⅞" wide. Cut the strip into 8 squares, then cut diagonally to make 16 triangles. (You may choose to cut additional black triangles to fill in other areas.)

Cut 4 strips 4" wide for the outer border. Piece if necessary, then cut into 2 strips 4" x 24½" and 2 strips 4" x 47½".

Table Runner Assembly

1. Piece 75 half-square triangles into squares. Make at least 16 squares using the solid black fabric triangles (the table runner in the photo has 17 squares with black triangles). Press seams to one side.

Sew.

Make 75.

2. Using the quilt photo for reference, lay out the squares in a random pattern on your design wall or a table, creating 4 black squares as shown.

3. Sew the pieced triangles into 15 rows of 5 squares each, pressing the seams of each row in opposite directions. Piece the rows together. Press.

4. Add the inner borders to the sides and then the top and bottom of the quilt top. Press toward the inner borders.

5. Add the outer borders to the sides and then the top and bottom of the quilt top. Press toward the inner borders.

6. Layer the table runner top, batting, and backing. Baste.

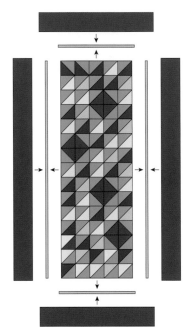

Let's Eat! **Table Runner Layout Diagram**

Finishing
Quilting

Ditch quilt around all of the triangles in the body of the runner, except those that form the black squares. Add decorative quilting to the black squares, which coordinate with the placemats. Use fruit shapes for the border quilting. I included many fruits that were not on the placemats. Fruit quilting designs are on pages 57–59

Binding

1. Sew the binding strips together. Press in half lengthwise.

2. Sew the binding to the top of the quilt. Fold the binding to the back and hand stitch in place.

Let's Eat! **Table Runner Quilting Designs**

Gallery

These eight quilts were selected because they showcase the quilting. In many cases the selected fabrics read as solids so the quilting designs show up clearly in the photos. In the detail photos you can see the quilting close up. Notice how the designs fill the space and leave spaces of unquilted areas next to the seam lines; this is another little pouf of fabric that adds to the beauty of the quilting. One of my goals when quilting is to fill up the space with the designs, creating as many poufs as possible. You really don't want a tiny flower or leaf in a great large space with large spaces left unquilted.

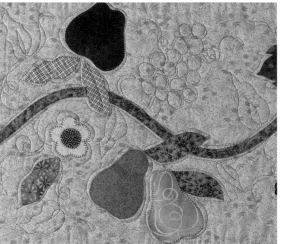

Here is a perfect design for adding fruit and leaves around the appliqué. In addition to the appliquéd fruit, more small fruit is in the fabric print, and quilted in the borders. (See Resources for pattern availability.)

Fruitful—Pears 'n' Apples, 42" x 58", designed and pieced by **Debra Haigh and Judy Cunningham, Camarillo, CA. Quilted by the author.**

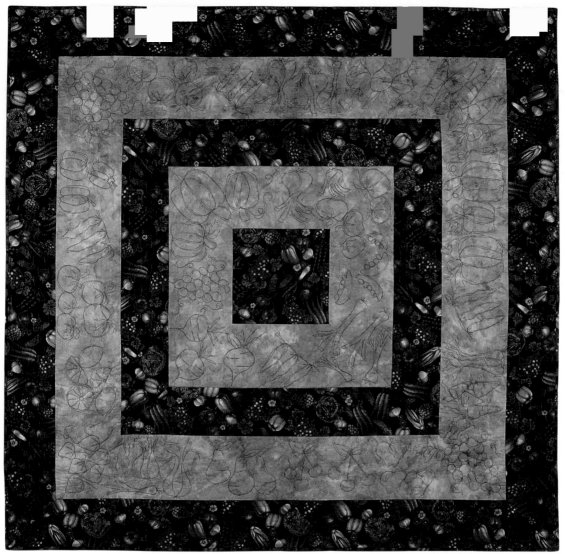

Fresh From the Garden Tablecloth, 70" square designed and pieced by Beate Nellemann, Pleasanton, CA, and the author. Quilted by the author.

Here is one of the very best inspiration fabrics I've ever found. It's "Bon Appétit" from Alexander Henry. The batik fabric between the print rows was a perfect almost-solid that was selected to showcase the quilting designs. How many food items in this print can you use for inspiration? The close-up photographs show the heavy-contrast thread and double stitching. The food fabric was quilted with chicken-wire fencing—to keep the critters out of the garden, of course!

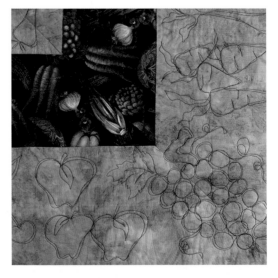

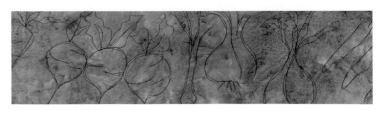

Cheerie Baskets, 66" x 70", pieced by Freddy Moran, Orinda, CA, based on a pattern by Sandy Klop, Walnut Creek, CA. Quilted by the author. (See Resources for pattern availability.)

Freddy's quilts are always bright, cheerful, and very colorful. Using lots of color creates a challenge to make the quilting visible. The body of this piece was quilted entirely with black thread, mostly double stitched. The black-and-white borders and lattice were quilted with red thread.

Quilting on the pieced peppers isn't really visible, but the almost solid-color border was a great place to quilt a couple dozen hot chilis all strung together. This is a small kitchen-type wallhanging. Wouldn't it look great next to a string of dried chili peppers?

Chili Peppers, 15" x 30", pieced by Hattie Bishop, Sonora, CA, based on the pattern in Ruth McDowell's *Pieced Vegetables*. Quilted by the author.

Japanese Garden, 44" square, pieced from a popular design by Maggie Hall, Tracy, CA. Quilted by the author.

The quilting on this piece is based entirely on the wonderful flowers and leaves in the fabric. Quilting includes a large poppy (see page 56) and a three-sided, jagged-edge leaf vines through the lattice strips. Black print squares are ditched, and the thread changes to coordinate with each of the fabric colors.

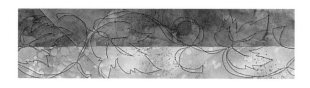

Quilting Sampler, 65" x 72" designed, pieced, and quilted by the author.

This piece was created just to showcase the quilting. When people look at a quilt, the piecing is usually the primary feature. This was my effort to make the quilting dominate the quilt, using just a bit of piecing and appliqué to create interest. The quilting includes the basic poppy (appliquéd flower), roses, lilies, and dogwoods, as well as numerous leaf vines. The designs are included in Chapter 4, Quilting Designs, with their inspiration fabrics.

Poppies Wallhanging, 38"x 48", an original design by Hattie Bishop, Sonora, CA, based on Ruth McDowell's piecing technique. Quilted by the author.

In this wonderful piece, Hattie's poppies float diagonally on a light-peach background surrounded by a border of pale green. The design creates perfect places to showcase quilting that mimics the poppies. The leaf border is based generally on the leaves of the large Chinese poppy.

Quilting Designs

Here are many of the designs I use in quilting, with some photos of the original sources of inspiration. You can create your own versions of these designs or use the drawings as a how-to guide. Pick a fabric from your shelf and try creating your own designs based on the flower, leaf, wheelbarrow, and so on. Your designs are not going into a museum, so don't reach for perfection. Just play! Use paper and pencil first, then practice on layered muslin. Dots on the illustrations indicate starting points.

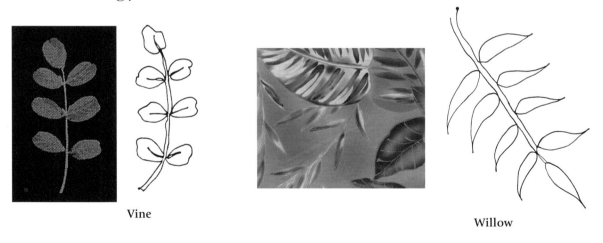

Vine

Willow

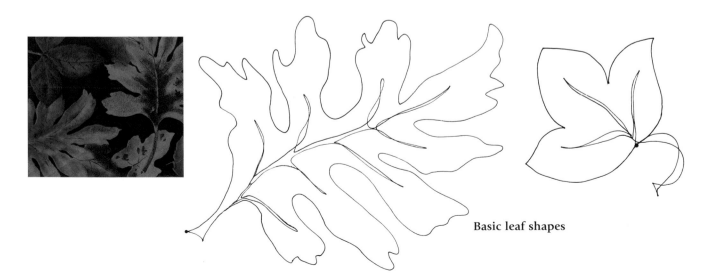

Basic leaf shapes

Sweet Gum leaf

Chestnut leaf

Susie's split leaf

Cattails

Rose leaves

Basic vine

Pine twig

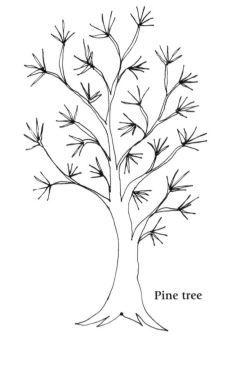

Pine tree

Pine cone

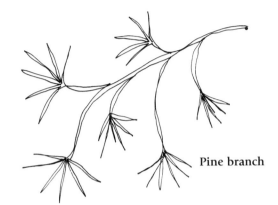

Pine branch

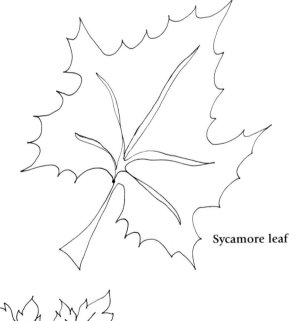

Sycamore leaf

Single ivy

Ivy border or lattice

Double ivy

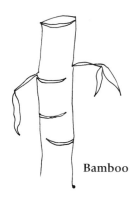

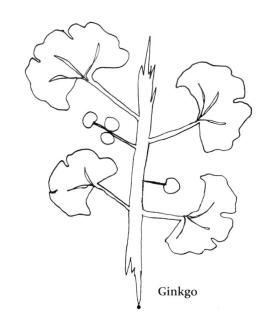

Bamboo

Ginkgo

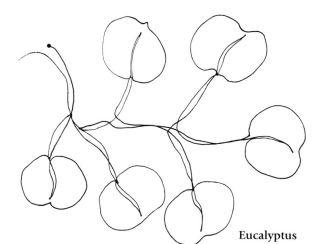

Eucalyptus

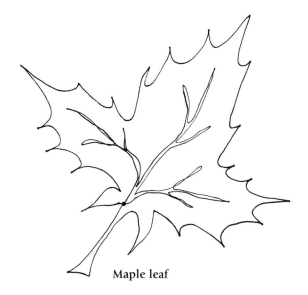

Maple leaf

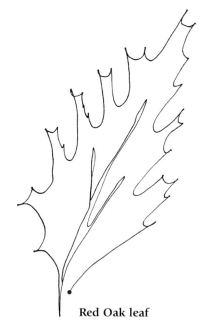

Red Oak leaf

Acorn

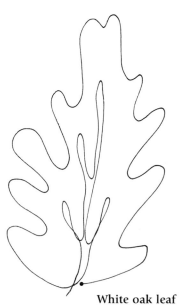

White oak leaf

Basic leaf shape

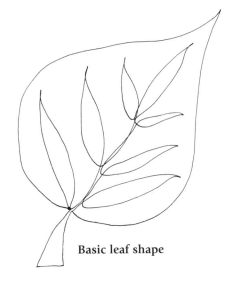

Basic leaf shape

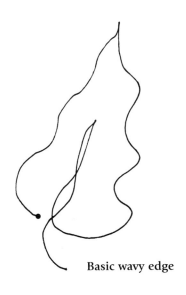

Basic wavy edge

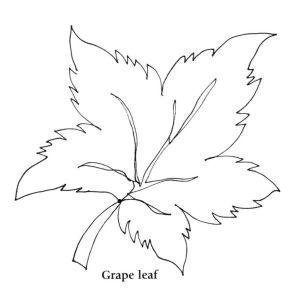

Grape leaf

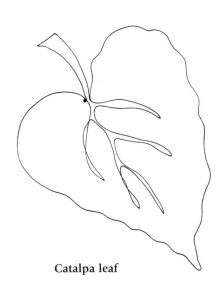

Catalpa leaf

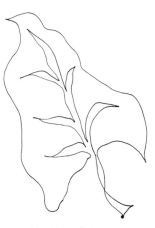

Basic leaf shape

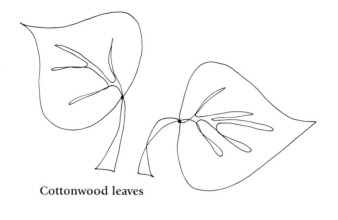

Cottonwood leaves

Nasturtium Leaves

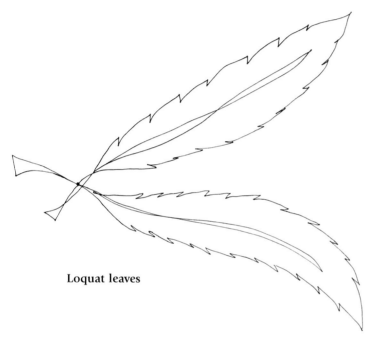

Loquat leaves

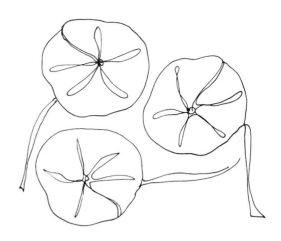

Holly

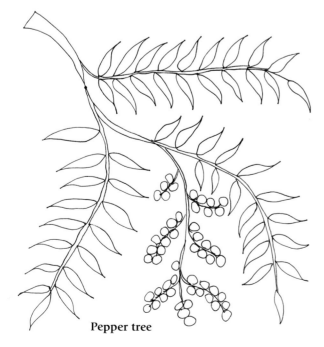

Pepper tree

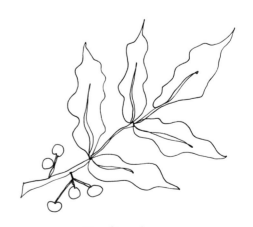

Carolina cherry

Fern 1

Fern 2

Fern 3

Pumpkin leaf

Philodendron

Basic flower

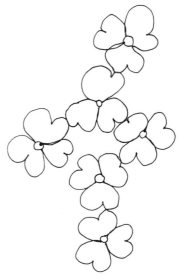

Oxalis for background or border

Rose; start with the center and build petals.

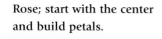

Single rose

Double rose; add leaves, sticks, and curls while stitching the second or outside row.

Basic tulip shape   Doubled tulip

Tulip cluster

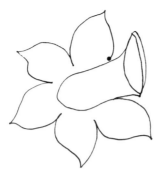

Single daffodil; Stitch petals first, then the trumpet.

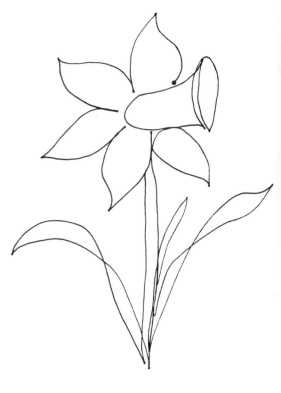

Double daffodils

Daffodil with stem and leaves

Lily; The first time through, create the basic shape.

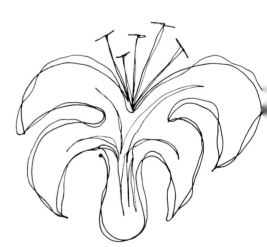

Lily; The second time through, ruffle the petals and add veins.

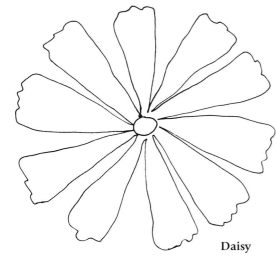

Doubled Daisy with two rows of petals

Daisy

Zinnia center; start with the center and add petals.

Zinnia

Zinnia with two rows of petals

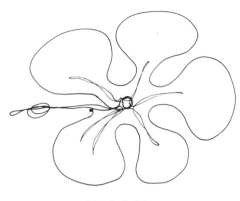

Single hibiscus

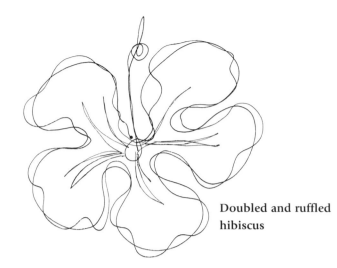

Doubled and ruffled hibiscus

Single iris

Doubled iris

Mariposa center; start with the center, then add petals.

Mariposa flower

Mariposa stem and leaves

Clematis center; start with the center and add petals, then veins.

Doubled clematis

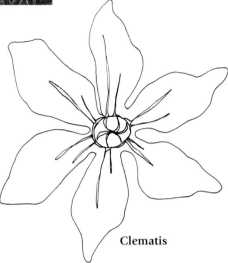

Clematis

Single flower

Doubled flower

Single dogwood

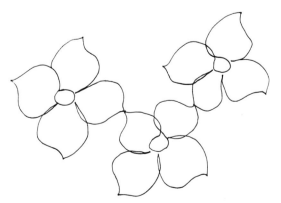

Dogwood cluster

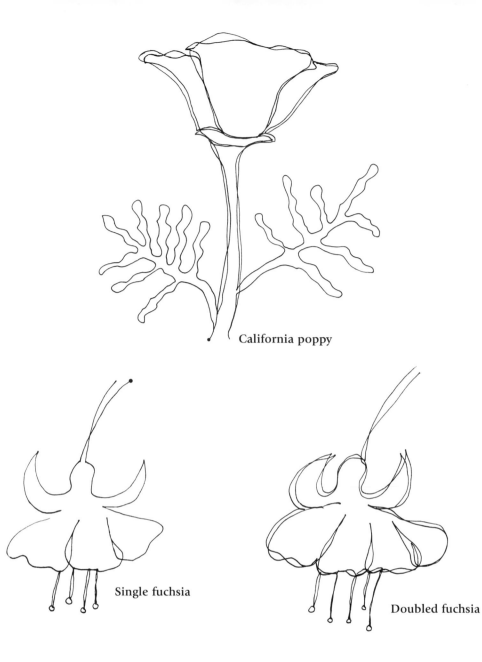

California poppy

Single fuchsia

Doubled fuchsia

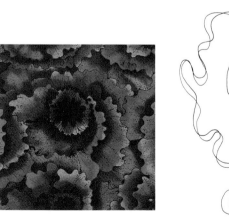

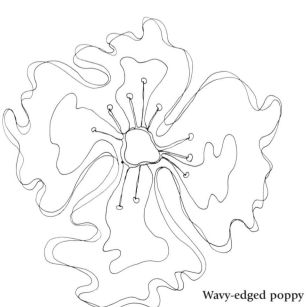

Wavy-edged poppy

Strawberries

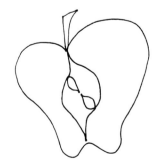

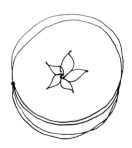

Apples

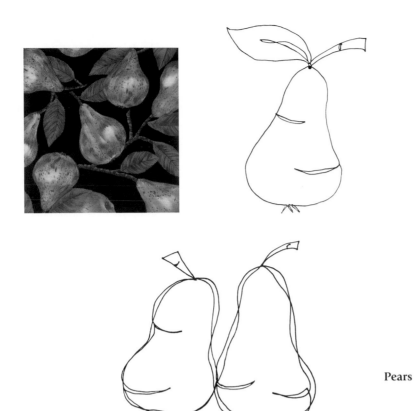

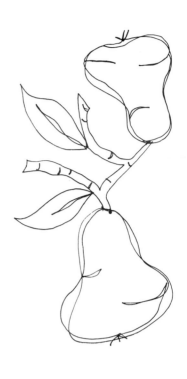

Pears

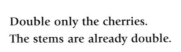

Cherries

Double only the cherries.
The stems are already double.

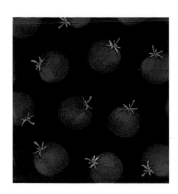

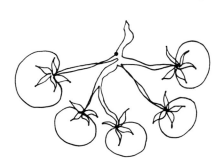

Tomatoes

Grapes

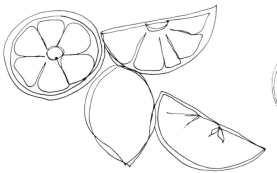

Lemons or limes

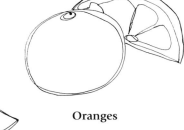

Oranges

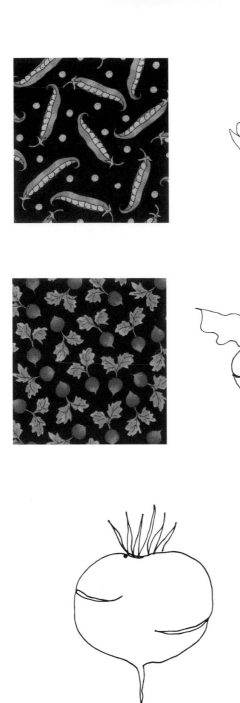

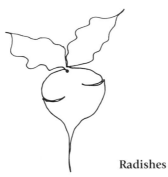 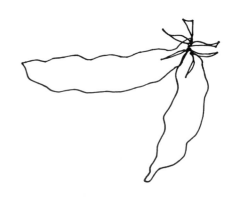

Peas

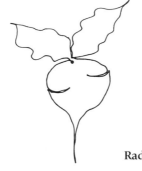 

Radishes

 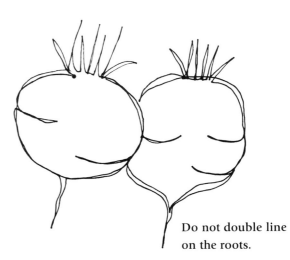

Beets

Do not double line
on the roots.

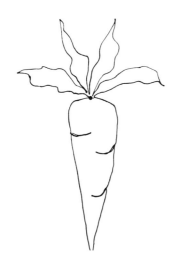  

Carrots

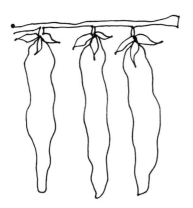
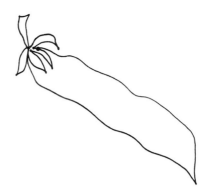

Beans

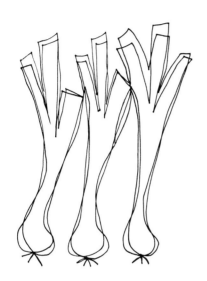

Scallions

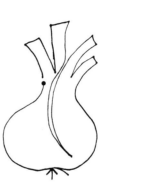
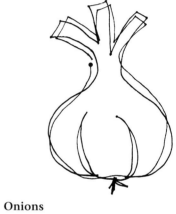

Onions

Green, red, and yellow peppers

Artichoke

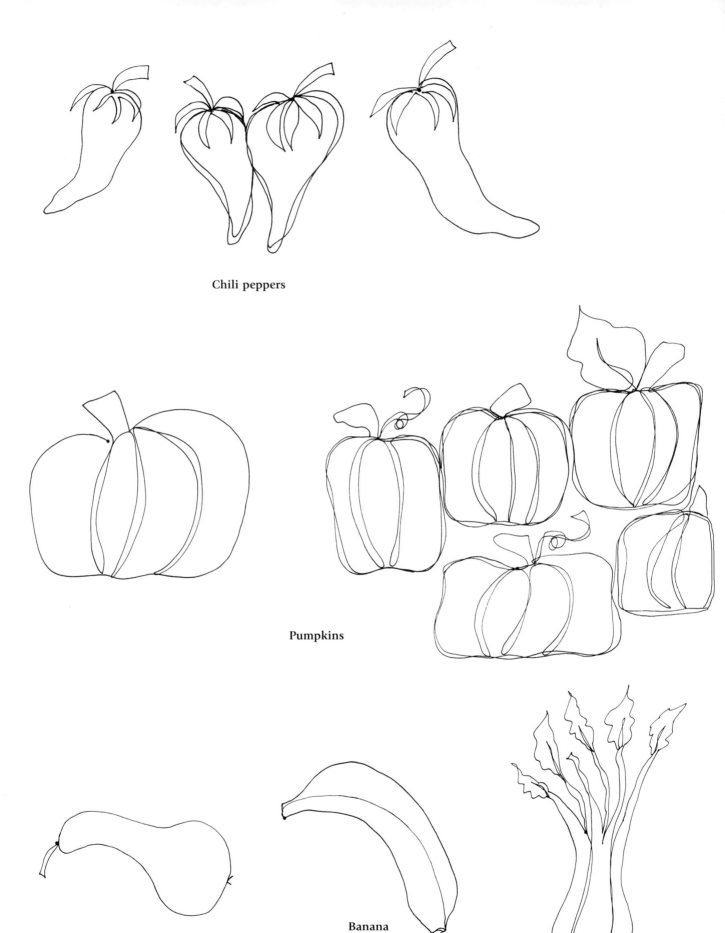

Chili peppers

Pumpkins

Squash

Banana

Celery

Resources

Aurifil's Mako® Cotton Thread
That Thread Shop
P.O. Box 325
Lemont, IL 60439
708-301-3172
Website: www.thatthreadshop.com

Quilt Gripper Gloves®
Toni Fitzwater/Quilting Unlimited
15203 South Elk Creek Road
Pine, CO 80470-8909
303-838-5122

Fruitful—Pears 'n' Apples Pattern (page 37)
Debra Haigh
11460 Sumac Lane
Camarillo, CA 93012

French Pantry Baskets Pattern
(used in Cheerie Baskets, page 39)
Sandy Klop/American Jane Patterns
64 Sandy Lane
Walnut Creek, CA 94597
925-947-6677

Subject Index

Quilting Designs Index

About the Author

Photo by Jerry Lee

Kathy learned to use a sewing machine at the age of 9 but focused her efforts on clothing construction rather than on quilting. She began quilting in 1982 when she attended a a quilting class with a friend. At first as a hobby, and then as a means of extra income, Kathy began to do machine quilting full time when she became self supporting in 1998. At the urging of friends, Kathy submitted her first book proposal in 2000 , and *Show Me How to Machine Quilt* was published in 2002. Kathy resides in the Pacific Northwest and lectures and teaches throughout the United States. You may contact the author through her website; www.MachineQuiltLady.com